# WE ARE ALL SLEEPING WITH OUR SNEAKERS ON

# WE ARE ALL SLEEPING WITH OUR SNEAKERS ON

## MATTHEW LIPPMAN

## POEMS

FOUR WAY BOOKS
TRIBECA

LIBRARY OF CONGRESS CATALOGING-IN-PUBLICATION DATA

Names: Lippman, Matthew, 1965- author.

Title: We are all sleeping with our sneakers on / Matthew Lippman.

Description: New York : Four Way Books, 2024.

Identifiers: LCCN 2023031706 (print) | LCCN 2023031707 (ebook) | ISBN 9781954245860 (trade paperback) | ISBN 9781954245877 (ebook)

Subjects: LCGFT: Poetry.

Classification: LCC PS3612.I647 W4 2024 (print) | LCC PS3612.I647 (ebook) | DDC 811/.6--dc23/eng/20230803

LC record available at https://lccn.loc.gov/2023031706

LC ebook record available at https://lccn.loc.gov/2023031707

This book is manufactured in the United States of America and printed on acid-free paper.

Four Way Books is a not-for-profit literary press. We are grateful for the assistance we receive from individual donors, public arts agencies, and private foundations including the NEA, NEA Cares, Literary Arts Emergency Fund, and the New York State Council on the Arts, a state agency.

We are a proud member of the Community of Literary Magazines and Presses.

*For David Weiss*

# CONTENTS

PART 3

# PART 1

# AS NATURAL AS FINLAND

A long time ago I walked into the courtyard of PS 1,
the museum in Queens, and the artist Pia Lindman
asked me to take off my clothes.
She said *sign this*
and I signed it
and I took my clothes off in the courtyard
and got into the portable sauna she constructed with oak slabs and tarp.
This was performance art
or public art
or the art of the body meets the rubble of the city.

I was round in the belly and the woman next to me was naked, too.
The sauna was big enough for two
and we were in there with a red sheet
preventing us from seeing each other naked.
But we were in the courtyard
naked
so we moved the sheet aside and said hello.
Our bodies saying hello.
This was not a sexual hello.
This was not us wanting to have sex in the courtyard of PS 1
known for its exhibitions of performance art.
We were not exhibitionists or performers.
We just wanted this to be Finland,
the way people in Finland
get naked and get in the sauna
like they take the dog out for a walk or,
fall down the stairs.

This was Queens but sometimes you have to stretch things out a bit.
I don't remember the woman's name but
want so badly to be naked in the world right now,
it hurts.
It's 8 degrees outside and it hurts
and if there was a sauna in my driveway I'd undress,
fall down the stairs, and hop in.
I'd invite the neighbors and their families
and the postwoman and the FedEx guy
and we'd all sit around sweating
and it'd be as natural as walking the dog in Finland.
Not the courtyard of PS 1
where everything was always a little too much about the mind anyway,
and not enough about the dry naked flesh,
bodies, lots of bodies,
sitting together at the round table of *sitting together*.

# LARRY LEVIS IS AN ALIEN THAT KNOWS GOD WILL ALWAYS BE 17

(for Michael Morse)

Larry Levis died when he was 49
in the space and time continuum of the arrested heart

and his accomplishments were too far out in the galaxy for me or anyone
    to name.
That is the problem with naming things we've done.

Sometimes they mean something to the woman in Alabama drinking
    her wine from Seattle
and sometimes they carry no weight whatsoever.

Michael told me when we were 29 that I'd love the poems of Larry Levis
and in time I got to love them.

In space I don't think I will ever adore them.
Space is a hard thing for me because I have not been able to figure out

how to move in it
from one end of the room to the other end of the room and kiss a woman.

Larry Levis died alone but his poem about God being 17 will always and
    forever
punch me in the face the way it did today

as I sat on the green cushions
wondering how I managed to get to this particular place

in the super-sonic super-slow pace that is my life, that is any life.
In all these lives we don't get to know many people

even though we talk to a lot of people. I want it to rain right now. Very
     badly.
As badly as I want it to kiss. For someone to kiss me.

I saw a movie earlier called *Monsters*, about aliens.
A man and a woman are traveling through the space and time of an
     infected area

called Mexico
to get to a non-infected area called America.

The reality is that everywhere is infected
because everything is beautiful.

The woman and the man want to kiss so badly
you can tell it hurts their bodies so badly.

At the end of the film, they are about to be eaten out of their human parts
by one of these creatures but then another creature shows up

and the two creatures, mate. In their mating they sound like whales and
     glow like
the northern lights.

Afterwards they vanish into the ether of physics and astrophysics, and no
     one is devoured.
But the man and the woman devour each other,

kiss each other like it means something under the lights of an abandoned
    gas station
with the mini-mart and all those chocolate bars.

In real life the actors are married and that's why their on-screen kissing
is the time it takes to get from the earth to the moon and

I wish Larry Levis
had been alive to see this movie with me and Michael.

Because it's a love story in a world where there shouldn't be love.
But there should always be love.

There should always be a room or a road that you have to travel inside of
    your body
and outside of your body

to get to someone else's body.
That's why God is always 17 even though Larry Levis's poem does not
    mention any of this.

That's because he died too young,
and if he did not know this, then I am telling him right now,

in the time and space of his death that keeps getting bigger and bigger
when guys like me try to obliterate sadness in the living room

working out the sounds we need to make like whales and monsters
so the person across the room knows to meet us somewhere in the middle.

And then when we have accomplished the work of getting there,
to the middle

you can watch us in our circle dance of love,
glowing red and purple and orange,

and can turn and kiss the person next to you whom you love so much
so that the kissing becomes the bending of light

the way that Einstein said that this kind of thing
happens in outer space

where the aliens spent so much time moving in their bodies
to get here

to show us how to do it and how always
to be 17.

## EMERGENCY ROOM

(for Rory Collins)

The other night I was broken.
My toe swollen.

Infected from the clippers.
From the air of old age so I said, *Babe, I'm off to the ER.*

And I was off,
in the car close to midnight.

The streets were empty, and the streetlights were angels
but they were really just angelic

I mean they were really just streetlights.
And I knew my toe would be okay, it was the solitude I was after.

The quiet night, the darkly lit streets, the streetlights in the moving car.
And it moved me to the ER as I limped inside,

the pain something I had known from youth, like broken love,
like that time she said *no* and I wanted her to be *yes.*

It was more of that pain, the heart pain that never makes you limp
but the infection swallowed up my foot and I sat in the waiting room to wait

right behind Elsa or was it Sarah or was it Eisenberg
and she howled in pain.

*Oh my God* and *I can't go on,*
every once in a while, throwing up into a blue bag,

every once in a while, falling to the floor
and most times in a wheelchair while her husband spread white hospital
    blankets

across her broken body. *Oh my* God and
*Why can't they help me?* Howling

until I fell asleep in my vinyl waiting room chair, sometime after midnight.
I did, fall asleep in that room, in that 1 a.m. hiss

until Elsa or Sarah or Mrs. Eisenberg woke me in shatters and screams
and some dude said to the husband, "Hey, is she gonna be okay?"

and get this, his hand on his wife's back, he said, "It's just a panic attack."
God almighty in heaven, I thought,

what a world we have built for ourselves that the body can be crushed by
    the spirit so simply.
But it was okay. It was Kate Bush. It was sweetness and terror

and the plastic partition between was enough of an explanation for this
    god almighty world
and I had found what I had wanted all along—the dark beautiful spirit
    of humanity—

and did not care how long it would take for the doctor to cut my toe open
to let the pus drain, the antibiotic to kick in, the night to swallow us all
   whole.

And when it was done, I limped back into the car and drove.
I could have driven all night into the dark oblivion of my suburban
   streets, my precious solitude,

but you can't do that
when there are people out there in waiting rooms and hospitals and
   nightclubs and classrooms,

screaming, *Oh my god oh my god,*
*please help me, please please please help me.*

## SOMETHING COULD COME OF IT CALLED *EVERYTHING*

What does it mean to be fucked in a good way?
Does it mean both people are just going at it
and the going at it is all butterflies and battlefield,
jackhammers or soup
dahlias and race car driving and sticking your toe in the bathwater?
Someone will probably read this and think I am a misogynist or a
     nationalist or an ageist.
Who gives a fuck?
The point is, what does it mean to get fucked in a way that feels good
and there is no mind involved,
no mind left
in the fucking?
That means that you disappear.
I want that.
I have never had this.
It's like what Isaac Luria said about the creation of everything—
that God had to disappear inside of God-ness
to make nothing
so something could come of it called everything.
Is that what a good fuck is?
Arriving into everything that is art, books, Ballantine ale, borscht,
and poems and piñatas and Pokémon and moons—you do the math.
It's just two bodies at the molecular level taking care of some kind of
     primal business
to feel something primal.
I must say, I wish my whole life was a good getting fucked.
I'm talking about drinking tea, making corn, driving to work, playing
     darts, picking lint,
saying *hello*—

the whole thing,

every little thing.

And that I could do it naked,

be naked even when my three-piece suit, all velour and Versace,

was covering my beautiful frame.

I wish we could all be fucked in a good way, every day and in every
moment.

Maybe then there wouldn't be any bad shit around the corner

where the darkness is,

all those lurking psychopaths in the front office,

in the Oval Office,

in the media office

in the office of ruin and despair,

kicking humanity in the head like, what,

it was meant to be tenderness or something?

## YOU WERE IN FRONT OF A CY TWOMBLY PAINTING

On the way home with the dog
I was reading your poem about Ryan Gosling at The Getty
where all the famous movie stars go
to make sure they are real people
and these two girls, right there on Tyndale St.,
they might have been sisters, were going at it.
Not like Ali and Forman, all Rumble in the Jungle hype, no.
Like UFC raging maniacs.
Right there on the front lawn.
And a boy, maybe their brother, maybe ET,
was watching them smash the shit out of one another
like he was watching an iris bloom.
These two were ripping each other's faces apart, tearing hair,
scratching eyeballs, and punching each other in the nose.
Tumble tumble smash.
And where were you Ryan Gosling, to save the day—
jump from your *Blade Runner La La Land*
spaceship to make it all safe again?
Oh, right, you were in front of a Cy Twombly painting
remembering that you are a person
who once could stand in front of a Cy Twombly painting
when you were just a person.
But these girls, man, they were fierce and falling.
Smashing one another to the grass then getting back up to do it all over
    again.
The dog didn't notice and the boy, he just stood there and straddled his
    bike, watching.
That's what men do when females fight. They oogle.
It was like he couldn't believe what he was seeing.

*Me neither* and then I wondered, do I step in?
Step in!
Because there was some blood and crying
that could have been laughing but was most definitely crying
like they couldn't believe it either, the girls,
tearing one another to shreds.
What the fuck is this? I thought.
Ukraine?
It looked kind of fun and their brother—he was definitely into it.
I stood there and I couldn't believe it because
I was half in your poem and half out of your poem
about vaginas and Ryan Gosling and he has two girls
and I have two girls but, shit, they don't fuck each other up like this.
*Should I stop them?* I asked the dog
but her face was in the urine stench of another canine
and the brother looked at me like *don't you dare, buddy,*
*this ain't your business.*
He must have been 12 or 9, so I kept walking.
The way your poem kept walking
and Ryan Gosling, he was as still as a motherfucker,
trying to keep the world out, except for his girls because he knows.
*They do they do they do*, these girls,
they rule the world.

## DOG ZONE

Me and the dog are in the dog zone.
She's on the grass ripping it to pieces.
Like she wants to get someplace quick.
Maybe the Village Vanguard.
Maybe an old age home.
*I'll join you,* I say,
but I'm too busy writing this poem.
I can't figure which is more important—the words or the dirt.
I can't figure out if anything is important.
I keep thinking about that kid killed in Chicago.
He was thirteen. I made the mistake of watching the cop body cam.
I saw Adam's face after he'd been shot.
Maybe he was already dead.
His eyes popped out of his eye sockets, supernovas
in suspended animation.
I can't figure out if it was a mistake, to watch that, to see that.
When he was on the grass
he couldn't get anywhere anytime soon,
stopped and
the dog is almost done with her digging.
Maybe she is just getting started.
Me? I don't matter anymore.
I never did.
Mattering is a quick case of getting somewhere quick.
To where you belong
or what you think you are—
a motorcycle enthusiast
or a man on the job, up the ladder, on the last step, waving the brush.
Adam Toledo was waving,

*No. Don't. Stop.*

Maybe he was on his way to Ohio.

We should all be so lucky to get to Ohio, without anyone running after us,

to halt our movement forward.

We should all be so lucky to be able to take our time, without worry, like
the dog,

who has been at it for 4 hours—paws and tongue and snout.

She'll get to her nowhere soon, but I'm afraid that's just a lie

because when they gun you down, fast,

it's all just dirt and words,

and there's no speed to speak of.

## AND THEN FAILED MISERABLY AT BEING SEXY

The buds came out overnight on the trees
and Kevin said, *It's like they came out overnight*
and so did the heat
but this can't be a poem about climate change in April
this has to be a poem about 80s pop music.
Daniel Nester would be happy about this
because he has a phonograph and all these obscure records from '83
when all of us from that era had just figured out that we could be sexy
and then failed miserably at being sexy.
The buds are sexy now.
They are so green even the dog notices
but do you know what the dog really notices,
Def Leppard.
*Photograph* is on the Spotify and all the birds want to do is fuck the
    whole band
in their big hair nonsense.
Imagine that?
Can you imagine that?
The little American robins
humping Joe Elliott till the night is blue with sorrow?
It's not sexy but sometimes it's sexy
and the sexiest thing I saw yesterday
was my friend Kevin, happy.
He was so happy he said, *It's like they came out overnight*, the green buds,
because he got a new job at 52
after a thousand years of believing he'd never get a new job at 43.
He was so sexy his face was green
and when I looked at the trees this is what I saw: Sexy Kevin,
in the buds of the trees,

in April, and last night the month wasn't the cruelest of them all
even though I love Eliot so much I hate his antisemitic guts.
But forget him.
Let's focus on sexy.
Last night I looked up and there he was, sexy Kevin,
green and blooming,
and this morning, the birds and Def Leppard are having sex
and Daniel Nester is writing his own poems, spinning out of his mind
on the tips of his Technics turntable
and all I can think is: it's good to have friends.

## COLOR UP THE ALREADY COLORFUL


Outside, up there in the sky, Orion's Belt hung like some crazy beauty.

So, I texted my kid, *Come out here now.*

But, she didn't.

She was in the shower or a space ship.

She was collecting butterflies and injecting oranges

with blue dye to color up the already colorful.

I was alone in the backyard.

I stood there trying to get some feeling out of me.

Looking up. Looking out. Diving in.

Orion's Belt and the North Star were talking.

I wanted my kid to come and join the conversation.

When she was younger and couldn't sleep,

we'd go out to the backyard and I'd show her Orion's Belt to calm her down.

It worked.

Sometimes it didn't work

so I bought glow-in-the-dark stars

and we pasted them to the attic ceiling

and when it got too cold outside we'd lay on the floor

and look up at them like we were in the backyard.

It worked and sometimes it didn't

and when it was 1 a.m.

I wanted to throw televisions out of the window

and drive garbage trucks through her room

to get her to sleep.

But, that was all a long time ago when I was a lousy dad

and in the backyard tonight

I was all alone, a miserable man,

trying to feel something.

*Orion, you bitch,* I said to it up there,

*take my hand and make love to me.*
But, I wasn't warm enough or cold enough.
The world does things to you sometimes
and you don't even know it.
You just feel it
and you are alone
and my kid came to me later and said,
*I got your text, but I was in my space ship circling around the shower with an*
*   orange in my hair. It's alright,* I said,
*Orion's Belt was out*
*and I wanted you to see it,*
*but the clouds came*
*and covered up the whole sky.*

## THIS MORNING WHEN YOU WOKE UP YOU NEEDED PETER TOSH

Sometimes it takes 30 years to listen to Peter Tosh.
You wake up one morning singing,
"I said I am that I am I am I am I am."
It comes out of nowhere like the stars come out of nowhere
and you must want to be what you are.
The last time you remember being what you were
you were listening to Peter Tosh
on a Greyhound bus to Ohio.
There was a woman in Ohio.
There is always a woman in Ohio.
You were everything that you were.
The fireflies told you that.
It took 8 years or 8 hours to get to Cleveland.
You listened to Peter Tosh the whole trip.
You had to flip the tape in the Walkman over and over
like the fireflies went over and over to tell you something.
They were there to tell you how beautiful you were.
You did not need the woman in Ohio.
You needed Peter Tosh.
This morning when you woke up you needed Peter Tosh.
Maybe it's the long endless bus ride of being stuck inside.
Maybe it's the endless amount of time that has spread out before you in
    timelessness.
That's what Peter Tosh is. Timelessness.
And you are getting in touch with timelessness because
it takes a long time to get in touch with timelessness.

# THE BIG WHITE AMERICAN SEGREGATION MACHINE

The moment I realized I was part of the big white American segregation
   machine
happened when I was having coffee with Nadia.
We were talking about private education.
She said, *I felt exhausted all the time in high school*
*because I am Black and I went to classes with too many skinny white girls.*
I said, *Private education sucks.*
Then I realized I was a teacher.
Not that I was a teacher.
That I was a teacher in a private school.
I took a sip of my iced tea.
Nadia took a sip of her coffee
and I got bummed out.
I think she was already bummed out.
The clouds had started to disappear and the rainbow-colored painted
   picnic table
where we sat was still wet from last night's rain.
She nodded when I said, *I am part of the problem.*
I didn't think I was always part of the problem.
I went to public school.
I taught in public school.
I hung out in public school playgrounds and faculty rooms and took naps
   on shitty rugs
in hallways with no doorways and copy machines
with no copying
and no paper
and plenty of broken paper clips.
I did that my whole life and then I came to live here.
But I don't think it matters where you live

except if you live in New York.
Nadia is moving to NY
because NY is *a thing*
even when everyone is wearing masks and Broadway is shut down.
It's a thing not because there are a thousand different faces
and religions and cultures.
It's a thing because you can see a dahlia on a street corner
talking to a mailman who has four thumbs filled with graffitied subway cars
and each one of those thumbs is a different planet called Saturn
telling the other one to fuck off
in the most loving of street corner ways.
I mean NY is a thing that is surreal
and so you have no choice
but to see everyone and everything like you have no choice
to go to the bathroom in the morning or
drink some water when you get thirsty.
I wondered if Nadia was moving to NY to be part of that
so I said, *Are you moving to NY to be part of that?*
And she said, *I don't want to live in any more bubbles*
*filled with wealthy white people.*
Or, something like that.
We hear what we want to hear to make sense of our own fucked up failings.
Like being part of the big white American segregation machine.
*Ah, fuck,* I said,
because the wet picnic table was making my pants wet
and I don't like being a private school teacher
even though there is a copy machine that makes copies
and they give you asparagus and steak for lunch.
Everyone should have that.

If everyone had that

I would be less bummed out.

Then Nadia and I said goodbye.

She was off to Avenue B to be out of a bubble

and I was off to my house to be with my kids.

When I got in the car, my pants wet from the rainbow picnic table,

I thought that maybe I would not go home.

That I would go to my school and quit my job and maybe that would be
    something.

Instead, I drove to the hardware store and bought some neon Krylon
    spray paint

and graffitied hearts and flowers on my thumbs

because I am still

and will always be

the most sentimental guy on the playground.

# PART 2

## SAFE HOME

I'm sitting on the floor watching Jackie Robinson die
or watching his funeral,
or he's stealing home
and he's dying into home.
I am sitting on my rug watching his funeral trying hard
not to look back.
There are all these people in dashikis and afros.
Everyone is Black and I can't find any white people in the footage
but there's a Florsheim Shoe store on the corner.

It's 1972 because it's always 1972.

The film is grainy and there are hundreds of cars and hundreds of people
maybe thousands of people
going home with Robinson,
and it's 2020
and we're all home, stuck inside our homes
while everyone else is outside
getting sick and dying. Red Barber said,
*The diabetes didn't kill him. It was the burden he brokered that ruined his body.*
My father said, *He played like he wanted to murder the wind,*

and my father's mind is dying
but he can still remember Robinson stealing home.
*I was there for that game,* he says, and I half believe him
and half picture him stomping on the plate
when Jackie slid that ballerina slide
and all of Brooklyn jumped on top of his body
with beer and brats and a sign that said *Welcome Home*

like he'd been in the foxholes at Bastogne
during the European Theater.
But his foxhole was right here in America, an American home,
in the American Theater of racism and hate
where no matter how many home runs he smashed,
line drives pelted,
he was still not anywhere close to being quarantined.

Today, in my American home with my American daughters,
I sat on my rug and watched his funeral procession
and cried so softly I thought I'd swallow my throat.
Stuck in their Covid Home
my children can't wait to run into the arms of their friends
and kiss them and hold them
and fall on top of them
without worrying about what microbe might tumble into their mouths.

That's why I call my father to ask,
*Did you ever see him play?*
*Yes,* he says, *every day*
*and the funny thing, Jackie was a Republican,*
*but at least I've got my acrylic paints to keep me from my mind.*
And I know his mind is floating around Ocean Parkway
with a stickball bat shooting out of his hands that is the magic wand of
    youth;
I know it's in Ebbets Field
watching Pee Wee Reese meet Robinson on the top dugout step
with the dirty uniform and the sweaty face
to shake his hand and, in that moment,

they've arrived,
they've found that warm place between men,
which transcends walls and doors and backyard fences.

That's what Rachel Robinson must have been talking about when she said,
*We always had home, no matter the brutality.*
It's the beauty of baseball—
that it can go on forever no matter the virulence:
there is no clock, there is no time,
there is no finite amount of days.
It is home, an infinite home,
one man barreling into the dust and disease of a broken world
that has since forgotten Florsheim shoes.
One man hurling himself straight ahead,
across the filthy, dirty plate of Ebbets Field
knowing damn well that he's anything but safe
as the ump jumps up
shoots his arms out across his chest
and sends the whole city of Brooklyn home, delirious,
still unable to believe what they just saw
while tonight my father sits in his living room squeezing his tubes of paints,
cerulean blue in his left hand
dove white in his right.

## WHAT'S GOING ON

(for Susan Browne)

This middle-aged blonde woman ripped off her mask
on the double yellow lines of Boylston Street and screamed, "What's
    going on?"
while the traffic shot past and the Prudential Building burned.
I looked up and two planes had hit it at the exact same time
that a sadness as big as an ocean
tore through the clean blue sky.
It was everywhere, and they weren't planes, they were swans,
come out of nowhere.
I ripped off my mask in the middle of Boylston Street and screamed,
"Where the fuck did you come from?"
like I was talking to the virus or the terror
or the blonde woman who had started to rip off her clothes.
There she was
tearing off her shirt and her pants,
scratching at her cheeks.
Someone ran out of Fenway with a baseball mitt to cover her privates
like baseball would be there to try and save the world at the end of the
    world,
but these days you can't even count on a nine-inning game.
She kept screaming, "What's going on?" over and over,
twirling around so fast it was making everyone dizzy.
Creating some kind of counter clockwise vortex that sucked the dude
    from Fenway right up, gone, and I'm thinking,
*Is this in all in your head?*
The Prudential Building burning in swan feathers and airplane fuel?
I couldn't be sure.
All I was sure of was that it smelled like New York
and I missed New York,

the city that makes the most sense
when you want to be in the whole world
at the exact same time that everyone else is in the whole world.
And maybe all of this was in my head.
Maybe I was seeing things. I didn't know.
What I did know was that I was on Boylston Street
at the exact same time that a consuming sadness was taking over.
We were all feeling it no matter what we saw or did not see—
everyone walking past with masks and gloves and no mouths
while the planes and swans flew into their faces
as our faces were trying really hard to figure out what was going on
and where to go when there were no answers to give to the woman in the
    street,
completely naked, screaming at the top of her lungs
into a sky so blue it wasn't going away.

## THERE IS A WORLD OUTSIDE THAT WANTS TO GO UP IN FLAMES

Sometimes I watch YouTube videos
of firemen putting out small cars on fire.
Right there in The Bronx.
No one's life is in danger.
There are no sirens or bullhorns or captains screaming, *Get these people back.*
8 guys for a little flare up.
I watch these images late at night
when the autumn is getting ready to piss everyone off.
Sometimes I have had 3 beers.
Sometimes 6 scotches.
Really, it's just a glass of water that has me seeing double.
My mind is so tired I can't remember the last time I lit a match.
The video reminds me that there is a world outside
that wants to go up in flames.
Whether that means atomic bombs
or autumn trees
depends on two things:
One, how beautiful your mind is on any given day.
And two, where your body moves in space
and how it gets there.
Most days I want my mind to be beautiful in flowers.
I want my body to move in space
close enough to other people
that they can hear me whisper words like *wick.*
But, who I am kidding?
I stay up late and watch videos of firefighters putting out fires on 125th
    Street.
The pedestrians in the videos walk past like nothing is happening.
They don't watch the fire like they don't say hello to the homeless

like they don't say hello to a neighbor.
And the world continues to burn in small spirits
and everyone is slightly charred and tender to the touch.
At some point in my life I wanted to be a firefighter.
So did the person next door and the stock broker
and the kid who punched the other kid on the playground.
I am sure of it.
It has to be true
because wanting to be a firefighter
is the only thing that keeps the world
from not being torn asunder
by flame, and ash, and an impossible, raging
heat.

# THAT VIBE FROM THE TV OF GERALD STERN

(for Scott Segal)

I just want to walk outside and listen to Ryo Fukui play his 1976 piano.
But the other day I saw Elton John play his 1977 piano on the TV.
It's this moment where he shows us how he made *Tiny Dancer*.
I told my daughter to watch it on her 2023 TV.
Then she got deferred from Northeastern
and my wife was so happy she danced around the kitchen
with all of her spoons gleaming, her can openers opening.
I stole that vibe from the TV of Gerald Stern
and his made-for-TV poem, *The Dancing*
about all those Jews killed in Treblinka and Bergen-Belsen
strewn in all the unknown ditches of Austria and the joy of Pittsburgh
that will never be a TV
the way New York City is Surreal TV
no matter the year, day, century.
It's the 21st century and I don't know where my mind is anymore,
not that I ever did,
but once in 1977 I wrote a letter to Elton that said,
*I love you I miss you I want to give birth to your 1969 piano*
*so the new songs will sound like the old songs*
because I knew he would only be a genius pop-song maker for so long.
That's what I told my daughter before she said listen to The 1975.
You see, everything has to have a timestamp on it
but what did prehistoric human do without time?
It was just the sun and the absence of sun.
I am glad in 2023 I get to watch 1977 Elton
figure out how to make *Tiny Dancer*
and so later I will go outside, naked, in the 12-degree cold snap.
I will wheel out my 2018 Samsung and hit YouTube
and listen to Fukui play *Early Summer*

in hopes that it will warm up the whole earth.

I know it will,

the way he slams so hard on the keys it's like flowers coming out of the
    hard earth, bougainvillea and daffodils,

and those other ones called black-eyed Susans,

they're so yellow

I don't care what year it is

or what kind of television you think will save your life.

## THERE WILL ONLY BE KANSAS

Someone mentioned the Thwaites Ice Shelf today.
I was drinking a gallon of bourbon and she said, "It's gone missing,"
which means that the sea will rise 10 feet
and there won't be any more coastal communities left.
There will only be Kansas.
But there I go again, being a racist or an ageist or a sexist or a nationalist.
I am so American my whole reference point about the rest of the world
is Kansas.
Why didn't I write, *There will only be Chad left standing, right there, in the
center of Africa?*
Because when the Thwaites Ice Shelf gets going in quick melt,
you can kiss Angola goodbye
just as quickly as you can say sayonara to Florida.
The other day I asked a roomful of 11-year-old children
what America was founded on
and they screamed out loud, all at once,
the way insane 6th graders are always screaming—
*freedom democracy McDonalds unity equality*, and I started laughing.
Really hard.
The way hyenas laugh
and then one kid got up on a desk and shouted *Guns*,
made a fake pistol with his fingers
and pretended to school-shoot us all dead
singing, like it was an old-time folk song,
*Don't forget to vote, don't forget to vote.*
That's when the fire alarm went off
and we peeked outside the door
looking for smoke
but there was no smoke,

there was just an enormous block of ice the size of Kansas

cutting a ravine through the hallway

and they were so crazy with middle-school lust

they jumped on the thing like it was a new roller coaster at Six Flags,

*The Doomsday Glacier,*

until everyone got sick to their stomachs, dizzy,

looking around for someone to hold them

in the cold ocean waters

rolling around their broken ankles.

## LEFT FOREVER LEFT

I spent some time standing in left field,
Just tucked
away in a corner surrounded by woods.
You get a right-handed batter with a mean cut, foul,
or a 315 shot,
and the ball is lost.
Today, I am the ball,
unfound in the woods
folded away in the corner of Brophy Field,
some run down middle-school baseball diamond
that is perfect.
Dandelions, like stars, everywhere.
Clippings from last week's mow, brown.
Home plate, solid,
and the pitcher's mound, too,
buried deep in the scorched earth.
I saw it from the road, pulled into the lot,
and walked out to left field.
It's the left field of Endy Chávez
and high school and summer camp.
It's the left field of the fascists and liberals and gun runners and gangsters
and little kids named Brenda and Dave and Javier and Marisol and Matthew
all of who stood out and waited and ran and dove and got bored and, mostly,
spent hours in the grass, watching the grass,
waiting on the sound off the bat, waiting for their moment.
Today, the world's moment is a carousel gone off the rails.
There is bird shit everywhere and everywhere we are lost.
Left field is not lost.
Left field is never lost.

It's always where it's supposed to be, in left.
Left of center, edge of the diamond
bordering the woods
where balls go gone
and sometimes little people, for a second,
disappear into the green to make the catch,
to retrieve the ball.
And when they emerge
sometimes they are still little people
and sometimes they've been gone so long
they return as grown.
Me, I stood out there today in the blistering heat with no baseball glove
    or cap
to speak of.
I was right where I was supposed to be,
on the team of the earth,
and the birds and the trees did their thing
as left did its thing, being left,
forever left,
no matter how many foul balls of history got swallowed up
into the forest primeval.

# BOUNCE

The FedEx truck hurtles up my street
like it's the Indy 500,
banks right onto Ainsworth
like it's going somewhere
as if there is anywhere to go.
My wife says stop being so dark
and I say *darkness*
and I say *sweetness*
and I say *slow down*
but the FedEx truck is doing 90 down South
then coming back with a busted muffler to introduce itself.
The packages rattle and fall off the back of the truck
like the children fall off the back of the truck.
I saw an Irish one and a Chinese one and a Jewish one and a Muslim
    one, bounce.
They were all bouncing,
like my daughter's Technicolor ball she got at Walmart to get her anger out.
Everyone is angry, and I sit here and watch the children collide off of
    parked cars,
bouncing, my daughter bouncing,
and I just sit here. All day long I sit here.
The FedEx driver is my friend, Ed, and I say, *Ed, slow down*.
I am trying to toss him a bottle of cold water.
It's so hot the tires on his truck melt. He's doing 75 up Bradford on rims
and the sparks are flying, ricocheting off the church steps and the clouds.
It's the 4th of July.
It's the 4th day of the year.
It's the 4th month of the lock down.
We're all pissed off and my wife says,

*Stop sitting around and do something.*
So, I bounce off my porch and run down the street
dodging the FedEx truck to retrieve the children.
I can't retrieve the children.
They are halfway into their own.
Their *owwness.*
I have tried so long to keep people safe by being kind.
Ed, on the 6th trip up this street, finally catches the iced cold 12 oz.
    Poland Spring,
blows me a kiss and more kids fall off the truck.
The short one and fat one and purple one and monster one and the one
    with pretty toenails and the smart one who knows math.
Maybe they'll figure out the algorithm to slow everything down, the
    anger, the lockdown,
the kind of meanness I thought didn't exist
till I saw my kid bounce her ball so hard
it hit the top of a mountain and, swear to God, knocked off all the snow.

## THIS WILL DESTROY YOU

(for Eliana)

My daughter does this thing,
it's this cool thing,
it's the thing that young people do when they figure out they no longer
    need you,
belong to you,
want anything to do with you;

she does this thing where she cooks up some turkey bacon,
makes up a bowl of berries, some toast, maybe a bagel,
hauls it all over to the window seat,
sits with a book, *The Pearl Thief,*
definitely not *Harry Potter,* she hates *Harry Potter,*
reading and eating,
all the spring air and light barreling into her like the guitar part
from a *This Will Destroy You* song
except there is no destruction anywhere to be found.
There's no decay or rot or horror.

There is only the cat
trying to get at her meat because he's hungry,
he's always hungry,
and if a bird flew into the house through the open window
he'd tear it to shreds
and everyone would get hysterical and start to scream
like the great wrath of God had finally come to pass.

But, before he can get his claws into the slab,
my daughter, the one who is all alone in her private spot
picks him up and places him quietly at another window

where he can smell the blood of the world through the screen,
and she goes back to her window
with her water and her breakfast
and is very much the person she is becoming
in solitude
and how beautiful it is;

remember how beautiful it was
when you discovered solitude,
thought about it,
thought, hey, this is kind of nice, I like this,
and then tried to get as much of it as possible
even when the world was pushing you to destroy yourself with other people.

## WE ARE ALL SLEEPING WITH OUR SNEAKERS ON

What am I supposed to do with all this white boy-ness?
Stuff it in a Glad garbage bag and be done with it?

Who cares anyway? As far as I can tell, I am still that kid
in Tough skins on the corner of Columbus and 94th.

It's 1974 and all we care about is the filthy candy store, Gus 'N Bernie's,
buying Now and Laters in our purple Converse.

We all had 'em. Pedro was the first. Then, Slade. Rosenblum, the middle
    one, got his next,
but they were red, and New York was a seesaw of murder, filth, and forensics.

We were kids with deep holes and patched ourselves up with fingertips
and Topps baseball cards. Through the grime you could still make out a
    flower—

a lily or iris or bougainvillea.
They had names. Javier, Schwab, Marisol, Angelina, Rebecca, Sarah, Leah.

How was I supposed to be *that* white back then when I am *this* white now?
A whiteness that didn't even know it was white.

I did not wake up and say to myself what the world was saying to me,
    *white boy.*
I woke up, some days, being the only Jew at the pizza place.

Because everything I do is privilege. Pick up the privilege phone. The
   privilege stapler.
The privilege Walkman with the John Coltrane privilege.

Because it doesn't matter if you grew up in low-income housing as a
   white boy,
you were, and still are, always, a white boy.

Then, yesterday, I read a book, *A Little Devil in America*, about Black
   Performance in America.
It's dedicated to Josephine Baker. It's by Hanif Abdurraqib.

There's an essay about line dancing and *Soul Train*.
When I was a kid in my purple white boy Converse, I loved *Soul Train*.

When I read the book, I thought about Angela because she's a Black
   American and loved *Soul Train*, too.
I wanted to buy her the book but then I thought that was a racist thing
   to assume,

that I could, should, would, buy her a book about Black Performance in
   America.
So, I said to her, *Angela, I read this book and I wanted to buy you this book,*

*A Little Devil in America, but I thought, that would be a racist thing to do.*
She said, *I understand. It's been that kind of year, but we talk.*

That's what she said, *we talk*, and maybe that's all that you need to do, sit down,
break bread, let it all hang out. But I'm not sure. I think that's too easy

and tomorrow I will be whiter than I was when I was a kid
in front of Gus 'N Bernie's joking around with Derek and Slade

eating Now and Laters because we didn't know anything else
and the thing with kids, until they reach a certain age, is that all they are, is present.

The thing about Don Cornelius was that he was always the coolest motherfucker in the room
even when Rufus and Chaka Khan were on in '74 singing *Tell Me Something Good.*

I knew it was good when I was saw it on my little black and white Panasonic
only because they sparkled, and Don Cornelius was the coolest motherfucker in the room.

I knew that, too, but most days, during some midday hour,
I close my eyes and say the Sh'ma.

*She-ma yisrael, adonai eloheinu, adonai echad.*
*Hear O' Israel, the Lord is our God, the Lord is One.*

But it's always the wrong time of day,
and it's the only prayer I know, and maybe my grandmother would be proud

even though she was a racist and I hated her for her racism,
even though she was from Transylvania

and there's that photo of the whole village, the entire shtetl,
wiped out by the Nazis and what do I do with that, white man?

I'm saying, once, in college, I walked across the quad on a spring day
with guitars falling out the sky and cherry blossoms falling off of guitar
    strings

and guitar strings making little ladders into our hearts
when a big white boy with football pads on his balls

threw a football at my head and called me *kikebitch*
like I knew him from the old neighborhood.

I did not know him from any neighborhood, real or imagined, and who
    was the white boy then?
I'm still listening to John Coltrane on my privilege Walkman trying to
    figure it out,

trying to have a conversation with Angela about all these little devils in
    America.
Who are they and how do we get them into our socks and under our arms

so we can lift off a bit from thinking we know anyone else before we can
    talk to them?
Is this *the something good* of Chaka Kahn

or why that riff rips me apart after all these years?
It's because when I was 9 sleeping in my purple Converse

hearing her sounds, I knew that Javier and Slade and Rosenblum
were doing the same thing,

we were all sleeping with our sneakers on, dirtying up the sheets
because it felt good and was fun,

and I say, *Grandma, I love you*
*but you need to leave the room, now,*

*with all the other racist, shtetl grandmas,*
*because it's not goddamn funny*

and I close my eyes and say the prayer and it sounds like home, but it's not,
it's some epic, disjointed body of work that is always there to remind me

that no matter how hard I try, white man that I am,
I will never be the coolest motherfucker in the room.

## THE END OF INTIMACY

When I saw S. at White Crest Beach I said, "What's up?"
She said, "We can't hug."
The last time we ran into one another
we held on for half an hour
before the traffic got really bad. She smelled like turquoise.
I smelled of barbershop.
At White Crest Beach the sand was stuck between our toes.
Earlier in the day
50 dolphins were stranded on Wellfleet Beach.
Some of them didn't make it.
50 volunteers came to help with blankets and water and muscles,
whatever it takes to refloat a large mammal.
When this was happening
I was at the top of White Crest Beach.
The sea went on forever.
S. went on forever. Her husband and son went on forever.
The dolphins, too, even the dead ones.
Later, my daughter and her friend saw one on the beach, washed up,
    graffitied,
in orange neon paint, "No. 3."
They said, "She was giving birth when she died."
They were so close to her they wanted to be midwives.
When I saw S. I wanted to hold her.
You can't do that anymore with old friends.
When you bump into them on White Crest Beach
you can't touch their bodies.
But, with the dolphins, you can touch their bodies, even with spray paint.
When they get stranded, you can go wrap your arms around them, take
    off your mask,

and whisper, "I got you."

That's why we need to grow dorsal fins and jump into the ocean.

This is the end of intimacy

and I am tired of running into people I can't touch.

Even strangers at the walk-up window at Dunkin' Donuts.

"Let me get a black coffee and a hand shake."

If we were dolphins, we could walk up to the Dunkin' Donuts window

and hold each other tight,

say, "I got you,"

then drop our mocha lattes into the sand

and not give a damn.

We'd have each other.

Even in the dead of winter,

we could hold on.

# *PART 3*

# HE CALLS HIS BAGELS SO/BAGELS

(for Daniel)

My friend makes bagels.
He sells them on the street in Bernal Heights.
On Cortland.
On Sundays.
On the tip of his tongue.
On the tops of the San Francisco hills.
Last weekend he sold six dozen.
One day he will have a bagel shop called *Schmear*.
He loves the word *schmear*.
It's a good word.
Do you know about good words.? They help you live better.
Like *vibration*.
Like an onion with the cream cheese and lox
the way Dan sits on his plastic chair and vibrates with his neighbors.
They shake and shimmee over the chive and the poppy,
the plain and the sesame.
They hum on the street
and turn the neighborhood into a neighborhood.
He calls his bagels *So/bagels*.
When we were twelve, we called him Sobel.
That's his last name from the shtetl,
before bagels were a thing.
Today, they are everything
and we all need one.
An everything with a schmear.
For our belly.
For our neighbor's belly.
For the belly of the world that tries desperately to get right, to feel better,
to bring something back to life
that we've all missed so terribly much.

# GEICO

We drove to the school to pick up the books.
They said don't get out of the car.
They said we will put the books in your trunk.
My kid was in the backseat and there were birds in her eyes.
I don't know what kind of birds.
They were the birds of her friends.
The ones she has not seen in weeks.

There were no cars on the road.
Driving to her school made me tired.
It made me want to take off my shirt and run into the woods.
My daughter was in the back seat.
She was lost at sea. She tried to follow the birds in her eyes
like sailors
to find their way on the waves.
Her friends were scattered all over the sky. In the trees.
they were screaming *Hello* but she couldn't touch them.

We drove to the school to get her books.
The new ones. For the new weeks.
The weeks that will lose their days.
Who knows what day it is.
Not even the cars know.
They just sit around parked
and don't crash into one another anymore.

# ROBERT GLASPER HAS ALL THESE FEELINGS ON HIS PIANO

after Robert Glasper

When Robert Glasper says *Fuck your feelings* he's not talking.
Oh, my bad, he's talking
but not with his mouth.
He's got his Yamaha keyboard on reverb amped up to 16
even though the Marshall Stack only goes up to 10
and I'm wondering if my feelings are supposed to be hurt
as a dude named Bob.
As a guy with short feet.
As a white boy.
That's what they used to call us on Amsterdam Avenue past 98th.
*White boy.*
I always brushed it off
no matter how many congas Ben P.'s dad had in his living room.
Rumor had it his father played drums with Paquito D'Rivera.
We didn't even know who D'Rivera was
or if he had any feelings that could change the world.
Robert Glasper has all these feelings on his piano
and I know he's looking to change the world.
Everything in his heart
is spilled over the piano keys
like some kid whizzed by on an old beat up 3-speed Schwinn
and dumped a bottle of Mountain Dew all sticky and sweet.
I can't remember the last time I was sticky and sweet.
Are my feelings supposed to get hurt when he tells me, "Hey white boy,
    fuck your feelings,"
or am I taking too much credit?
He's not even talking to me.
He's talking to the neighborhood, to the county, to the system of circuits,
    plugs, prods, pistols, patrolmen, and panic

that seeps and seams through these streets.
We all have too many feelings.
Just put away your guns and let's get on with it.
Pianos are better anyway.

## HELLO KINDNESS

I think you we were talking about Ratso from *Midnight Cowboy*
played by Dustin Hoffman in your poem about bad men.
Didn't Hoffman get slammed for being inappropriate with women?
What is wrong with him, anyway, with men, anyway?
Then, everyone gets shot.
I just read about two women in Baton Rouge, college kids,
gunned down by bullets and cars and beer and balls.
I have 2 daughters. Last night
the basement door blew open.
When I woke up the rain was shouting inside,
*let me out let me out*
like a person in fear for their body.
The first thing I did was to check on my kids,
walked into their rooms to make sure it was just the wind,
not some man with a rubber hose or large knife, come to wreak havoc,
that blew open that door.
One of the women in Baton Rouge was
shot in her car.
I can't believe I have to write that line,
*shot in her car.*
Her father said, *Something has to change in the minds, in the culture.*
I don't want to be that father who has to say things like that.
No father wants to be that father.
How does one change the culture, the mind culture, the heart culture?
How does that happen?
More flowers?
More iced tea?
More ballet and modern dance?
Maybe more oboe and piano.

I know soft things like tissue paper and the way someone else's hand
can be a velvet cloth if you understand how to be kind.
It's simple and a cliché but fuck you, I don't care, just be kind.
I am sorry to say *fuck you* but sometimes I have to say it to be kind,
it's the root of kindness,
you say it and then you are soft, so say it,
once twice three times
and then go check on your kids or your cat
or your kindness, say, *Hello kindness,*
*I am here and I want to hold your velvet hand*
*through the dark movie theater with the sticky, crunchy floors.*

## SHE LOVES THE EARTH WITHOUT CURSE WORDS

Natalie says, "Dad, quarantine's good for you."
I say, "Why?"
She says, "You only said the F-word twice last week."
Fuck. I'm losing my *shwing*, I think.
Then she steals the Spalding from right out of my cold hands
and lays it in the hole with a left hook.
Every day we go out to the driveway and shoot hoops.
We go out and smell the moon and feed the stars.
Every day we watch the new cardinal land on the fence
and each day we give it a new name.
Yesterday it was Francine.
The day before that it was Francisco.
Tomorrow it could be Amira.
The point is I don't look at CNN or the *Daily Guardian* or reports
    coming out of Italy or Detroit.
I don't read *The New York Times* or *The New Yorker* or *The New York Post*
    or *Boston Globe*.
I just go outside with my daughter
and bounce the ball.
I know this makes me a bad man
but according to her
I've only said the F-word twice in the last 7 days.
Maybe that means I'm getting dumber.
I don't care that I am getting more stupid.
It makes my daughter happy
even though, for the past year, every time I've said the F-word
she got a dollar.
Truth is, she loves money. Today, I realized,

cardinals and stars are more important to her than cash.
A clean mouth makes her quiet in the way that a 20-dollar bill doesn't.
And, of course, the left hook, outside of 12 feet,
nothing but net.

## A SENTIMENTAL SHOT AT HUMANITY

Kerrin, I don't know why I address you in this moment,
perhaps it's because you are in Vermont and I used to summer camp there
when I was as whole of a lad as a lad could be
with all of those trees and silences
creating prairies in my blood.
It's March and my children are growing up.
The Avett Brothers song *Laundry Room* is on the Spotify
and it occurs to me that all I have been doing for 18 years is laundry.
The white load. The colored load.
The load of bills and anxiety and iced tea
and late nights with the kids
when they couldn't fall asleep
and were throwing up bile and aspartame and nightmares.
But today, in March, I turned 58
and the children are slowly and quickly loading up the car and taking off.
The Avett Brothers have a song called *I and Love and You.*
They sing, *"Brooklyn Brooklyn take me in."*
A long time ago I thought Brooklyn was France
and then it took me in
and I made it my home.
We birthed our first child there
although I did no birthing of any kind
but I sure as shit held her up to the Cobble Hill streetlights when she
    was born,
said, *Look at us now*, and here we are,
the way time is a motherfucker,
and I don't even miss myself from back then.
The other night Michael said, *What's going on?* I said,
*I am learning how to pay attention.*

He said, *Huh,* because it made sense to say.

We can say a thousand things to one another, Kerrin,

and sometimes all someone needs to utter is *huh*

and the cosmos just goes tumbling out and tumbling out and keeps on
tumbling.

I miss you Kerrin, and that's really why I address you in this poem

and everything makes me cry.

Can we say that in a poem?

What if Major Jackson read this poem?

Or Jorie Graham?

Or dead Gerald Stern?

Would they think it was a sentimental shot at humanity?

Who cares anymore?

I am 58 and all I have is a good heart.

The Avett Brothers know and right now, I like that.

I know if they read this poem, we'd drink whisky and get out the
mandolins

to make some noise.

That's why, Kerrin, I address you in this poem.

We get out the mandolins to always make some noise

and my daughter, at this exact moment, is upstairs doing her own load of
soiled sheets.

It's hers and I have no more quarters.

The truth is I could write this poem forever, just keep it going,

that's my talent,

but it's probably time to stop and whisper *Brooklyn* into the ears of my
iced tea,

an homage to some faraway place that let me do the family laundry in
Laundromats

owned by people named Lucy and Franklin,
people who used to bend down with me, get close to the hot dryer,
and sing to the tumbling clothes,
*I and love and you.*

## CRYING AND SUNSHINE

If a thing can make you cry then it is a thing, a thing with a capital *T*,
or a capital *Th*
and that is what your poem has done to me, for me,
made me sit in the kitchen at the white table
and weep
but we are not supposed to write about crying in our poems.
I don't care anymore. All I want to do is cry in our poems.
I sit here in the 50-degree sunshine and *Here Comes a Regular* is on the
    Spotify.
Remember that song, Susan?
Remember The Replacements?
They were always drunk on cheap beer
and I am drunk now on your poem
and how it makes me feel lots of things about absence and presence.
Yes, my kid is off to college and I worry that it will be hard for her,
all those hours alone with strangers, the cold winter air taking turns on
    her heart,
on her dorm window.
She is a sensitive one with lots of sensitivities and her stereo, I fear,
will not be enough to keep them at bay.
This is her beauty, those sensitivities, and I worry like any father
and I want nothing more but for her to make her strength out of blood
    and honesty
so she can be a regular,
the way all of us are regulars,
the way all we do is
*here we come.*
That's all I want for her to manage, her regular-ness in her stupendous-ness
so she will be able to sit alone in her college room and know

that there is love enough to hold her like your poem has held me,
in my crying and sunshine.
That's what regulars have most.
Crying and sunshine.
Your cat, Fifi, knows, and so does your man, Kenneth,
when you sit down at your regular table
with your regular coffee
and remember what it was like to feel like you were more than regular.
It takes a long time to figure out that you are a regular,
even when you win the Nobel Prize for Poetry,
the Universal Award for Scientific Research,
and walk down the aisle to get your trophy and your check
and everyone is clapping and shouting: *Here she is, here she is,*
*here comes the regular.*

## SCREAMING MUSCLES OVER BROKEN HURDLES

When I walked into the Reggie Lewis Track and Field Center
for my second vaccine
I could feel my muscles shift
a little bit off the bone.
There were no lines for the inoculation.
The place went on forever.
I imagined young people running the 100 meters,
and pole vaulting,
and screaming muscles aching over broken hurdles.
I imagined sweat on cheekbones and some 21-year-old, in the corner,
    vomiting
after her close to a regional record sprint.
There were people in the stands urging the athletes on
and big screens with neon numbers, clocks, timers, timed out.
You could taste the heat and the winners and the losers
and the muscles on my arm were relaxed
when the RN, Jill, stuck the needle in my bicep
and, for a second, I thought I might be free,
that the world and all the folks in the Reggie Lewis Track and Field
    Center, might be free,
shot up, out of a canon, at the sound of the starter pistol, released.
More than that, though, I felt like I belonged,
that we all belonged,
each and every one of us sitting in the *observation area*
to make sure we did not vomit, or pass out, or sweat out, or bleed out.
We all belonged to each other, for each other,
and I did not want to leave.
I did not want to return to the street of my life
or my family

or my instincts
or my failures and flops and fidgets.
I just wanted to stay, belonging, me and us,
and all the kind and decent people
in the Reggie Lewis Track and Field Center,
getting our shots
and then being observed,
observing one another
to make sure that no one fell ill,
fell off their chair, to the ground,
in this cavernous building that could hold so many of us
under its big, belly of a roof
like it should always be
no matter the oval of the hour or how far away
the finish line.

# FUCK POEMS

At 4 a.m.
I got a rejection note from a literary journal.
They said, Get outta here with your crazy poems.
Rejections don't bother me but this one bothered me.
Not because it was from a particular magazine or editor.
The rejection was like the core of a rotten orange being extracted
from a different time zone.
When I read the rejection
I did not feel relevant anymore
and, in my mind, this is why the literary journal did not want to publish
my poems.
In my mind the poems must not have been short enough, Jewish enough,
Black enough, white enough,
LGBTQ enough,
too cis-male enough, not Prince enough,
or open-hearted enough,
or, too open hearted-enough,
not love enough, or, love in the wrong way enough.
Whatever it was that made the editors hit the reject button
was not of my concern, though.
What was of my concern was why I was up at 4 in the morning in the
first place.
My 11-year-old had vomited earlier
after eating peanuts and for a second, we wondered if she would stop
breathing.
She did not stop breathing
but she was worried about having her larynx close up on her.
She couldn't sleep enough.
We lied in bed together, not sleeping enough.

Hold my hand, she said.

Can I put my head on your shoulder? she said.

Then she would sit up and shake from her fear.

A real shaking, the kind you can't make up.

The kind your body just does when everything is out of sorts

and the ego does not matter.

Will my throat close up? she asked.

Will the sky close up? she asked.

Will I close up? she asked,

and there were not enough words that I could find to help.

There were not enough words to string together in little magical
    tightropes

to help her from her body,

to quiet her body from thinking

it would stop breathing.

## ON OUR BEST DAYS

(for Jay)

We are all people just walking around.
You cross the street; they hop the curb.
Some dude runs down the path.
We're making time. Flicking lint. Eating pears. Dialing phones.
The cat stands at the door. Wants to run after the bird.
We're just walking up stairs and through parking lots
to get our fix.
To hang out on the corner and be alone.
Some of us watch cars race by with dying brothers.
Others rake leaves.
We hold ourselves. We warm ourselves.
We love our neighbors for having more money than we have.
We want to give them some of our time.
Some days, there is no time.
We walk around confused and in our polka-dotted shorts.
We walk around in our anger and sadness
and can't seem to sit down at the same table and eat the pot roast.
It's a beautiful pot roast.
We should all eat the pot roast.
What else is there but the fork and the spill?
Because it does not matter if you believe in flying saucers
and she believes in Frida Kahlo.
We have to share the sidewalk
like we have to share the path
when the mountain bikers race down it, too close to our children,
who almost get hit by the spinning wheels, fall down
and smash their heads against the rocks.
Our hearts are so big.
You can feel it right now, can't you?

The cat feels it.
The worm feels it.
We're just walking around.
Some of us fall onto the concrete.
Some of us pick up the person who has fallen.
One day it will be us that falls
and there will be a nice folk in yellow chiffon
to come and prop us up against the mailbox,
brush us off—the blood and dirt—
even if it means they get stinking filthy dirty
right before letting us go.

# ACKNOWLEDGMENTS

*Pine Hills Review*

*The Lost Pilot Review*

*American Poetry Review*

*The Literary Review*

*The Massachusetts Review*

*About Place*

*The Cortland Review*

*Sixth Finch*

*Ovenbird*

*Pleiades*

*A Gathering of Tribes*

*Boston Review*

# *GRATITUDES*

I would like to thank:

Michael Morse, David Weiss, Mark Bloom, Rebecca Lippman, Melvin Lippman, Carol Lippman, Amy Saltz, Mark Heyert, Dan Sobel, Naomi Laguana, Sharky Laguana, Billy and Tommy Laguana, Steven Morse, Aaron Tillman, Ed Pavlic, Virginia Konchan, Susan Browne, Tina Cane, Kerrin McCadden, Juan Felipe Herrera, Henry Israeli, Nicole Lipson, Bridget Bell;

Paul Rozenfeld, Kevin Bolan, Adina Astor, Michael Weissman, Pam Adelstein, David Borden, Nicole Kokolakis Borden, Darcy Gould, Alex Gould;

Courtney Shepard Muller for her generosity;

and, my beautiful and totally excellent family—Rachel, Eliana, and Natalie.

# ABOUT THE AUTHOR

*We Are All Sleeping with Our Sneakers On* is Matthew Lippman's 7th poetry collection. He has won numerous awards for his poetry. He lives and works in New England.

PUBLICATION OF THIS BOOK WAS MADE POSSIBLE
BY GRANTS AND DONATIONS. WE ARE ALSO GRATEFUL
TO THOSE INDIVIDUALS WHO PARTICIPATED IN
OUR BUILD A BOOK PROGRAM. THEY ARE:

Anonymous (14), Robert Abrams, Michael Ansara, Kathy Aponick, Jean Ball, Sally Ball, Clayre Benzadon, Adrian Blevins, Laurel Blossom, Adam Bohannon, Betsy Bonner, Patricia Bottomley, Lee Briccetti, Joel Brouwer, Susan Buttenwieser, Anthony Cappo, Paul and Brandy Carlson, Dan Clarke, Mark Conway, Elinor Cramer, Kwame Dawes, Michael Anna de Armas, John Del Peschio, Brian Komei Dempster, Rosalynde Vas Dias, Patrick Donnelly, Lynn Emanuel, Blas Falconer, Jennifer Franklin, John Gallaher, Reginald Gibbons, Rebecca Kaiser Gibson, Dorothy Tapper Goldman, Julia Guez, Naomi Guttman and Jonathan Mead, Forrest Hamer, Luke Hankins, Yona Harvey, KT Herr, Karen Hildebrand, Carlie Hoffman, Glenna Horton, Thomas and Autumn Howard, Catherine Hoyser, Elizabeth Jackson, Linda Susan Jackson, Jessica Jacobs and Nickole Brown, Lee Jenkins, Elizabeth Kanell, Nancy Kassell, Maeve Kinkead, Victoria Korth, Brett Lauer and Gretchen Scott, Howard Levy, Owen Lewis and Susan Ennis, Margaree Little, Sara London and Dean Albarelli, Tariq Luthun, Myra Malkin, Louise Mathias, Victoria McCoy, Lupe Mendez, Michael and Nancy Murphy, Kimberly Nunes, Susan Okie and Walter Weiss, Cathy McArthur Palermo, Veronica Patterson, Jill Pearlman, Marcia and Chris Pelletiere, Sam Perkins, Susan Peters and Morgan Driscoll, Maya Pindyck, Megan Pinto, Kevin Prufer, Martha Rhodes and Jean Brunel, Paula Rhodes, Louise Riemer, Peter and Jill Schireson, Rob Schlegel, Yoana Setzer, Soraya Shalforoosh, Mary Slechta, Diane Souvaine, Barbara Spark, Catherine Stearns, Jacob Strautmann, Yerra Sugarman, Arthur Sze and Carol Moldaw, Marjorie and Lew Tesser, Dorothy Thomas, Rushi Vyas, Martha Webster and Robert Fuentes, Rachel Weintraub and Allston James, Abby Wender and Rohan Weerasinghe, and Monica Youn.